Cultures Around the World

the World

Jeanne Dustman, M.A.Ed.

D1137852

Consultant

Caryn Williams, M.S.Ed.
Madison County Schools
Huntsville, AL

Image Credits: p.19 (right) Blend Images/Alamy; p.22 (top) Bjarki Reyr MR/Alamy; p.22 (right) Brian Yarvin/Alamy; p.21 (bottom) Christine Osborne/World Religions Photo Library/Alamy; p.26 (right) GoGo Images Corporation/Alamy; p.9 Paul Springett C/Alamy; p.11 (top & middle) The Bridgeman Art Library; p.8 Alex Livesey/Getty Images; pp.18–19 Andre Vogelaere/Getty Images; p.12 (bottom) Keren Su/Getty Images; p.7 (top) Matias Recart/AFP/Getty Images; p.25 (top) Nick Laham/Getty Images; p.25 (bottom) Torsten Blackwood/AFP/Getty Images; p.19 (left) The Granger Collection, NYC/The Granger Collection; pp.15 (top), 26 (left), 28–29 (background), 29 (top & bottom) iStock; p.20 (right) imagebroker/Gabrielle Therin-Weise/Newscom; p.10 (left) Vandeville Eric/ABACA/Newscom; p.23 (top) Wikimedia Commons; all other images from Shutterstock.

Teacher Created Materials
5301 Oceanus Drive
Huntington Beach, CA 92649-1030
http://www.tcmpub.com
ISBN 978-1-4333-7361-9
© 2015 Teacher Created Materials, Inc.

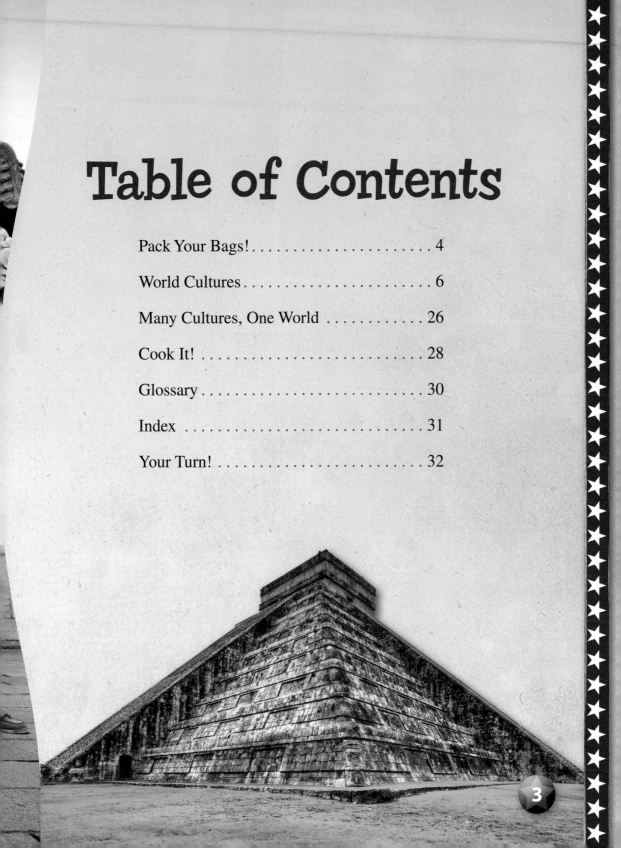

Table of Contents

Mexico

Brazil

Brazilians march to a World Cup match.

Pack Your Bags!

There are many countries throughout the world. Each country has its own **culture**. Culture is the set of **customs** and **beliefs** that is common to a group of people. In this book, we will visit 10 countries and learn more about their cultures.

It is good to learn about other cultures. It helps us know and respect people from around the world. It can be fun, too! It is exciting to learn about celebrations in China and Brazil. And it is fun to see the kinds of music people dance to in Russia and the Philippines (fil-uh-PEENZ).

Russia

Italy

Israel

China

India

Philippines

Kenya

Australia

All of these cultures make up our world. Each culture is unique. It is part of what makes each country special. But we are all part of one world. And we love to celebrate the ways we are the same and the ways we are different—together!

This dancer celebrates Chinese New Year.

The Pyramids of the Sun and Moon were built in Mexico long ago.

World Cultures

Each country in the world has its own unique culture. Learning about each country enriches our lives.

Mexico

Mexico's culture is rich in color and **tradition** (truh-DISH-uhn). People who lived in Mexico long ago made vivid art. Dye from plants was used to make colorful clothing. They studied the stars. And, they loved to play sports! Tamales (tuh-MAH-les) were a favorite at meal times. They drank foamy chocolate drinks. They even built grand temples that still stand!

This girl celebrates Mexico's independence.

Tinga Time!

Tinga is a Mexican favorite! It is shredded chicken mixed with a special, thick tomato sauce. It is served on warm, crunchy tortillas.

Today, tamales and sports remain favorites in Mexico. Mexican culture is still full of colorful celebrations. On September 16, Mexicans really have fun! This is Mexico's **Independence** (in-di-PEN-duhns) Day. There are parades and feasts! The smell of fresh salsa and tinga (TING-guh) fill the air. The colors of Mexico's flag—green, white, and red—can be seen all around.

Brazil

Brazil is the largest country in South America. Every spring it has a huge party! **Carnival** is a wild bash that is four days long. There is dancing and music. There are games and parades. People dress in bright costumes. It is a time for them to be happy and to forget their problems. Carnival is the most famous celebration in Brazil. It is so famous that it is known around the world!

Brazil's soccer team is world-famous, too. Brazilians love soccer! The whole country watches when its team plays in the World Cup. People wave flags and wear green and yellow. These are Brazil's **national** colors.

World Cup

The World Cup is a soccer tournament that happens every four years. There are 32 teams from around the world that play in the Cup. Brazil has won the Cup five times!

These two Brazilian soccer players celebrate after winning the World Cup in 2002.

Parades during Carnival are colorful.

Italy

Italy has a long history. The Roman Empire began in Italy long ago. It was once the largest empire in the world. The Colosseum (kol-uh-SEE-uhm) was built in the city of Rome during this time. If you go to Rome, you can visit the ruins of this great building.

Vatican City is at the heart of Rome. It is where the pope lives. He is the leader of the **Catholic** Church.

Many great artists came from Italy. One great artist was Michelangelo. He painted the ceiling of the Sistine (SIS-teen) Chapel. Today, many people travel to Italy to see his artwork.

Italy's culture is also known for its food. Pizza and pasta are tasty foods from Italy. Many grapes and olives grow there, too.

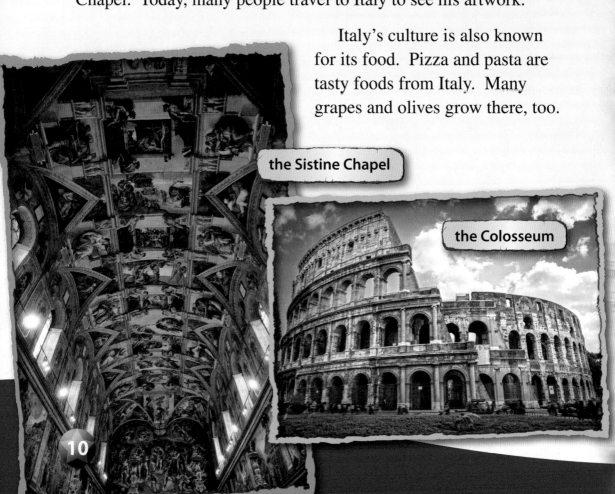

the Sistine Chapel

the Colosseum

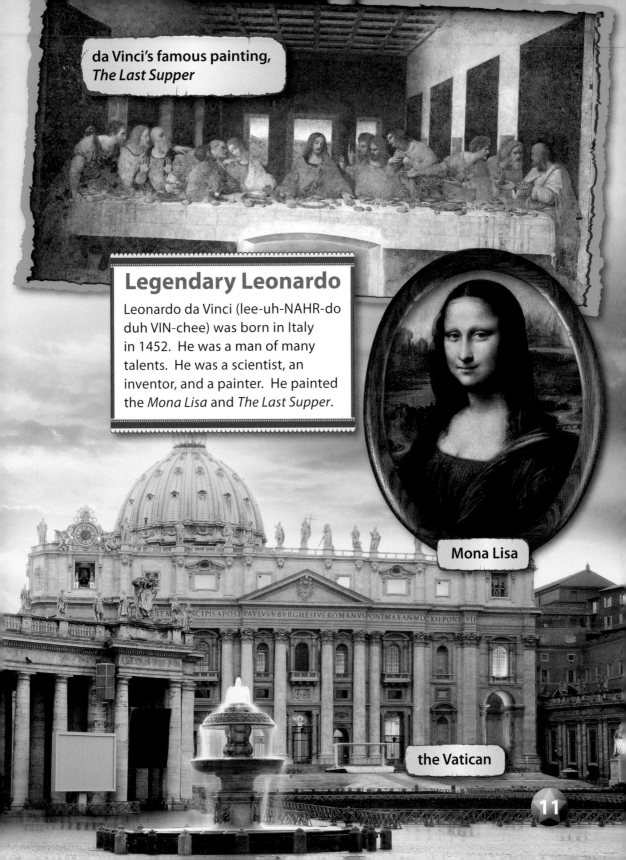

da Vinci's famous painting, *The Last Supper*

Legendary Leonardo

Leonardo da Vinci (lee-uh-NAHR-do duh VIN-chee) was born in Italy in 1452. He was a man of many talents. He was a scientist, an inventor, and a painter. He painted the *Mona Lisa* and *The Last Supper*.

Mona Lisa

the Vatican

11

Masai (muh-SAHY) tribe in Kenya

Kenya

Kenya is a large country in Africa. There are many **tribes** in Kenya. Each tribe has its own culture. Music and dancing are part of these cultures. Each tribe loves to share stories, too. They pass down their beliefs and customs through these stories.

These Kenyans celebrate with dancing and music.

Lots of Languages

There are more than 60 different languages spoken in Kenya! Most people who live in Kenya speak more than one language.

Kenyan warrior

Kenyans have many celebrations. Tribes decorate their bodies with paint, feathers, and beads. They wear costumes, play drums, and dance. The start of the rainy season is a big celebration. So is Jamhuri (jam-hur-EE) Day. This day comes every December 12. It **honors** the day that Kenya became its own country in 1964. Speeches are given and people dance. There are also feasts and parades!

Israel

Israel (IZ-rey-uhl) is a small country. Jerusalem (ji-ROO-suh-luhm) is its capital city. Many people think it is a **holy** city. People have fought to live on this land. Countries still fight over Israel.

Most people in Israel are Jewish. When Jewish boys are 13, they are seen as men. They have a celebration called a bar mitzvah (MITS-vuh). When Jewish girls are 12, they have a bat (BAHT) mitzvah. These celebrations are important in Jewish culture.

Israel is home to the Western Wall. This stone wall has held an important place in Jewish culture for a very long time. Visitors write prayers on pieces of paper. Then, they slide the paper between stones in the wall.

People celebrate a bar mitzvah in Israel.

The Holy City

Jerusalem is a holy city for three **religions**. Muslims believe that Muhammad (moo-HAM-uhd) rose to heaven from the city. Jews think that the Messiah (mi-SAHY-uh) will appear in the city one day. And Christians believe that Jesus Christ died and then came back to life in Jerusalem.

Prayers are stuck in the Western Wall.

Russia

Russia is the largest country in the world. It crosses two continents! Part of Russia is in Europe, but most of it is in Asia. Moscow is Russia's most populated city. It is also the capital. It is very bright and colorful! The Kremlin is in Moscow. It has five palaces and four **cathedrals** (kuh-THEE-druhls). If you visit Moscow, be sure to dress warmly. It is usually very cold in Russia.

Russia has a creative culture. It is known for its music and writers. Many famous artists came from Russia, too. Some artists decorate eggs. They put paint and jewels on eggshells. Peter Carl Fabergé (fab-er-ZHEY) created his first egg in 1885. People now call these fancy eggs Fabergé eggs.

Beautiful Ballet

Ballet (ba-LEY) is a big part of Russian culture. If you are a kid in Russia, you might become a ballet dancer. Many Russian girls and boys learn ballet.

Fabergé egg

St. Basil's Cathedral in Moscow

the Kremlin

17

This parade celebrates Chinese New Year.

China

China is one of the oldest and most populated countries in the world. Chinese culture honors hard work and learning. Chinese people understand that they can learn a lot from their elders. Often times, grandparents live with their families. This way, they can help teach and guide the kids.

This painting shows a Chinese papermaker in 1643.

Chinese family

Ni Hao

In China, the most common spoken language is called *Mandarin* (MAN-duh-rin). To say "hello" in Mandarin, you say "ni hao" (nee how).

Long ago, China was a leader in science and math. It also led the world in technology. The Chinese invented things such as paper and gunpowder.

But the Chinese like to have fun, too! Chinese New Year is a big celebration. There are parades with fireworks and paper dragons.

India

India is a large country in Asia. It has over a billion people! Religion is an important part of life in Indian culture. There are many different religions in India. Hinduism (HIN-doo-iz-uhm) is the main religion. Hindus believe in many gods. There is also Buddhism (BOO-diz-uhm). It was started by an Indian prince. He became known as the Buddha (BOO-duh).

India is also home to lively art forms. Many films are made there every year. The films often include singing and dancing. Many of these films are made in the city of Mumbai (mum-BAI). People call this city "Bollywood." They say it is the Hollywood of India.

A statue of the Buddha sits at a temple in India.

Bollywood movie poster

Hindus pray at a temple in India.

That Is Spicy!

Curry can be a food or a sauce in Indian cooking. Curry is a mixture of many spices.

Philippines

The Philippines is a nation of more than 7,000 islands! The islands are in Southeast Asia. Rice **terraces** are a special part of Filipino (fil-uh-PEE-noh) culture. They are striking to see. But it takes hard work to keep the rice growing. The terraces help control the water flow. The skills for farming the terraces are passed down to each **generation** (jen-uh-REY-shun).

Rice is in most Filipino dishes. Pancit (pawn-SIT) and léchon (LEECH-uhn) are favorite dishes. Pancit is usually served at birthday parties. Pancit is thin rice noodles. It is mixed with vegetables and meats. For big parties, léchon is served. This is a roasted pig!

A family eats traditional Filipino food.

pancit

léchon

rice terraces

Tinikling

Dancing is popular in the Filipino culture. One folk dance is called *tinikling* (tin-uh-kuh-LING), or the bamboo dance. It tells the story of a bird moving in tall grass.

Sydney Opera House

Australia

Australia is the only country that is also a continent. People have lived there for at least 50,000 years! Its native people are called *Aborigines* (ab-uh-RIJ-uh-neez). These people probably came from Asia long ago.

Australian culture is rich in art and music. One form of their art is made with many dots. The dots form a picture. They also make art by carving stones. They create music with a didgeridoo (dij-uh-ree-DOO). This is a long tube you breathe through to make sound.

This Aborigine plays a didgeridoo.

Women compete in the Cricket Australia Women's Cup match in 2004.

Sports Fans

Australians love sports! They spend a lot of time playing sports outdoors. They enjoy surfing and swimming. They like to play cricket and rugby, too!

These performers at the Sydney Opera House rehearse for opening night.

Music is also an important part of Australian culture. In Sydney, Australia's capitol, there is a famous opera house. Opera is a kind of singing. People from around the world come to see operas performed there.

Many Cultures, One World

Cultures are formed by the past and present. They are shaped by where we live. They change over time. Our world is filled with many unique cultures. It is always good to learn about the different ways in which people live. This helps us see why each country is special. It also reminds us to be respectful of others who are different.

We may celebrate different holidays. But we all celebrate. We may eat different foods. But we all eat. We may dance to different music. But we all dance. We each have our own unique cultures, but we are also part of one world culture.

This young Mexican dancer performs in a traditional costume.

Cook It!

You can learn a lot about a culture through its food. Choose a culture from this book that interests you. Research and read about the different foods that are unique to that culture. Then, have an adult help you cook a traditional dish for your family and friends.

pancit from the Philippines

tamales from Mexico

This family cooks different types of food together.

Glossary

beliefs—feelings that something is true or right

Carnival—a festival held before Lent that includes music and dancing

cathedrals—the main churches of an area

Catholic—relating to the Roman Catholic church

culture—the characteristics of everyday life shared by a group of people in a particular place or time

customs—ways of behaving that are usual among people in a particular place

generation—a group of people born and living during the same time

holy—respected as sacred or connected to a god or a religion

honors—treats with respect and admiration

independence—freedom from outside control or support

national—relating to an entire nation or country

religions—organized systems of beliefs, ceremonies, and rules used to worship a god or group of gods

terraces—flat areas on the side of a hill that are used for growing crops

tradition—a way of thinking or doing something that has been done by a particular group for a long time

tribes—groups of people who have the same language, customs, and beliefs

Index

Your Turn!

World Explorer

Do some more exploring! Find a country that interests you but was not featured in this book. Research and learn more about its culture. Then, write a new chapter for this book about that culture. Be sure to include descriptive words and details in your text. Then, find colorful pictures that will make your chapter more appealing to your readers.